THE **ESSENTIAL** BUYER'S GUIDE

TRIUMPH

350 & 500 Unit Twins

3TA, 5TA Speed Twin, T ~~~~~~~~~~ 100SS,
T100 Tiger, T100S, T ~~~~~~~~~~ 00R, TR5T,
T100D Daytona ~~~~~~~~~~ 57-1974

Your marque expert:
Peter Henshaw

VELOCE PUBLISHING
THE PUBLISHER OF FINE AUTOMOTIVE BOOKS

Essential Buyer's Guide Series
Alfa GT (Booker)
Alfa Romeo Spider Giulia (Booker & Talbott)
Audi TT (Davies)
Austin Seven (Barker)
Big Healeys (Trummel)
BMW E21 3 Series (1975-1983) (Reverente, Cook)
BMW GS (Henshaw)
BMW X5 (Saunders)
BSA 500 & 650 Twins (Henshaw)
BSA Bantam (Henshaw)
Citroën 2CV (Paxton)
Citroën ID & DS (Heilig)
Cobra Replicas (Ayre)
Corvette C2 Sting Ray 1963-1967 (Falconer)
Ducati Bevel Twins (Falloon)
Ducati Desmodue Twins (Falloon)
Ducati Desmoquattro Twins (Falloon)
Fiat 500 & 600 (Bobbitt)
Ford Capri (Paxton)
Ford Escort Mk1 & Mk2 (Williamson)
Ford Mustang (Cook)
Ford RS Cosworth Sierra & Escort (Williamson)
Harley-Davidson Big Twins (Henshaw)
Hinckley Triumph triples & fours 750, 900, 955, 1000,
1050, 1200 – 1991-2009 (Henshaw)
Honda CBR600 Hurricane (Henshaw)
Honda CBR FireBlade (Henshaw)
Honda SOHC fours 1969-1984 (Henshaw)
Jaguar E-type 3.8 & 4.2-litre (Crespin)
Jaguar E-type V12 5.3-litre (Crespin)
Jaguar XJ 1995-2003 (Crespin)
Jaguar XK8 & XKR (1996-2005) (Thorley)
Jaguar/Daimler XJ6, XJ12 & Sovereign (Crespin)
Jaguar/Daimler XJ40 (Crespin)
Jaguar Mark 1 & 2 (All models including Daimler 2.5-litre
V8) 1955 to 1969 (Thorley)
Jaguar S-type – 1999 to 2007 (Thorley)
Jaguar X-type – 2001 to 2009 (Thorley)
Jaguar XJ-S (Crespin)
Jaugar XJ6, XJ8 & XJR (Thorley)
Jaguar XK 120, 140 & 150 (Thorley)

Kawasaki Z1 & Z900 (Orritt)
Land Rover Series I, II & IIA (Thurman)
Land Rover Series III (Thurman)
Lotus Seven replicas & Caterham 7: 1973-2013 (Hawkins)
Mazda MX-5 Miata (Mk1 1989-97 & Mk2 98-2001) (Crook)
Mercedes-Benz 280SL-560DSL Roadsters (Bass)
Mercedes-Benz 'Pagoda' 230SL, 250SL & 280SL
MGA 1955-1962 (Sear, Crosier)
MGF & MG TF (Hawkins)
MGB & MGB GT (Williams)
MG Midget & A-H Sprite (Horler)
MG TD, TF & TF1500 (Jones)
Mini (Paxton)
Morris Minor & 1000 (Newell)
New Mini (Collins)
Norton Commando (Henshaw)
Peugeot 205 GTI (Blackburn)
Porsche 911 (930) Turbo series (Streather)
Porsche 911 (964) (Streather)
Porsche 911 (993) (Streather)
Porsche 911 (996) (Streather)
Porsche 911 Carrera 3.2 series 1984 to 1989 (Streather)
Porsche 911SC – Coupé, Targa, Cabriolet & RS Model
years 1978-1983 (Streather)
Porsche 924 – All models 1976 to 1988 (Hodgkins)
Porsche 928 (Hemmings)
Porsche 930 Turbo & 911 (930) Turbo (Streather)
Porsche 944(Higgins, Mitchell)
Porsche 986 Boxster series (Streather)
Porsche 987 Boxster and Cayman series (Streather)
Rolls-Royce Silver Shadow & Bentley T-Series (Bobbitt)
Subaru Impreza (Hobbs)
Triumph Bonneville (Henshaw)
Triumph Stag (Mort & Fox)
Triumph TR7 & TR8 (Williams)
Triumph Thunderbird, Trophy & Tiger (Henshaw)
Vespa Scooters – Classic two-stroke models 1960-2008
(Paxton)
Volvo 700/900 Series (Beavis)
VW Beetle (Cservenka & Copping)
VW Bus (Cservenka & Copping)
VW Golf GTI (Cservenka & Copping)

www.veloce.co.uk

For post publication news, updates and amendments relating to this book please visit www.veloce.co.uk/book/V4755

First published in September 2014 by Veloce Publishing Limited, Veloce House, Parkway Farm Business Park, Middle Farm Way, Poundbury, Dorchester, Dorset, DT1 3AR, England.
Fax 01305 250479/e-mail info@veloce.co.uk/web www.veloce.co.uk or www.velocebooks.com.
ISBN: 978-1-845847-55-5 UPC: 6-36847-04755-9

© Peter Henshaw and Veloce Publishing 2014. All rights reserved. With the exception of quoting brief passages for the purpose of review, no part of this publication may be recorded, reproduced or transmitted by any means, including photocopying, without the written permission of Veloce Publishing Ltd. Throughout this book logos, model names and designations, etc, have been used for the purposes of identification, illustration and decoration. Such names are the property of the trademark holder as this is not an official publication.
Readers with ideas for automotive books, or books on other transport or related hobby subjects, are invited to write to the editorial director of Veloce Publishing at the above address.
British Library Cataloguing in Publication Data – A catalogue record for this book is available from the British Library.
Typesetting, design and page make-up all by Veloce Publishing Ltd on Apple Mac. Printed in India by Replika Press.

Introduction
– the purpose of this book

Triumph twins of the 1950s, '60s and early '70s exude sexiness, glamour and sheer desirability. As a result, prices of the 650s and 750s (especially the Bonneville) have risen beyond the reach of many enthusiasts. However, the smaller Triumph twins – the 350s and 500s – have all the style of their bigger brothers, but in a slightly more affordable package that's very easy to ride and enjoy.

This book is a straightforward, practical guide to buying one secondhand. It won't list all the correct colour combinations for each year, or analyse the bikes' design philosophy – there are excellent books and websites listed at the end of this book that do all that – but hopefully it will help you avoid buying a dud.

The smaller Triumph twins – known collectively as the 'C' series – were very popular in their day. Around 75,000 were built, with plenty having survived. All the qualities that made them popular when new make them a good classic bike in the 21st century. C series Triumphs are physically small, light and easy to get on with. Performance is good enough for modern conditions (as long as you keep off motorways), spares aren't expensive, and the bikes are good on fuel. Additionally, some features that haven't stood the test of time so well can be upgraded with modern fixes that won't detract from the classic looks.

A Tiger 90 takes the sun at Brighton beach – it has all the style of bigger Triumphs.

The 16-year production run really encompassed the shift in motorcycle culture from a commuter-based market to a leisure-based one. The first of the line, the Twenty-one of 1957, was intended as clean, undemanding and fuss-free transport – the same was true of the 5TA which followed. But within a few years, increasingly youthful buyers demanded more power and raunchier looks – the Tiger 90 and 100 fitted the bill, with the high-pipe T100C adding off-road style. The T100C was more street-scrambler than pure off-road machine, but the final TR5T of the early 1970s was a stab at a proper trail bike. As for the twin-carburettor Daytona, that was the sportster of the range, descended from racing success at Daytona Beach in Florida.

Triumph 500s like this one can make a good first classic bike.

Whichever of these C series Triumphs you go for – whether it's the mild-mannered 3TA or fast and revvy Daytona – you'll have the classic Triumph twin experience in a bike that's very easy to just get on and ride.

Just one word of warning on originality: When new, most of these bikes were owned by young and enthusiastic owners who, in the words of author Matthew Vale, loved to "thrash, crash and modify." He's quite right, and the result is that few Triumph 350/500s still have the exact specifications they left the factory with, unless they've been very carefully (and expensively) restored. In short, don't worry too much about 100% originality when buying one of these – the important thing is to buy one, and enjoy it!

Thanks go to Nik Askins of H&H Auctions for his help with pictures, to Dave at Somerton Motorcycle Engineering, to Eion Warner and to the absent owners of all the bikes I snapped whilst they were parked! Also thanks to Justin Harvey-James who has compiled the C series website www.triumph-tiger-90.com.

NB: References in this book to the 'drive' and 'timing' sides of the bike refer to left and right respectively, as seen when sitting on the seat.

Contents

THE ESSENTIAL BUYER'S GUIDE™ CURRENCY

At the time of publication a BG unit of currency "●" equals approximately £1.00/ US $1.70/Euro 1.24. Please adjust to suit current exchange rates using Sterling as the base currency.

1 Is it the right bike for you?
– marriage guidance

Tall and short riders
Good news for smaller folk, as by modern standards these are small, lightweight bikes. No bigger than a modern 250, they can actually feel cramped for six-footers. The seat height is a modest 30in (762mm), and at around 350lb (160kg), they don't weigh much.

Running costs
Modest again, thanks to reasonable spares prices (see below) and fuel consumption. The single carburettor 350s and 500s shouldn't have much trouble averaging 60-70mpg, though the twin-carb Daytona will use slightly more.

Maintenance
Make no mistake, any bike from this era needs more TLC and sympathy than modern machines. You'll need to change the oil every 1500 miles to maximise engine life, and keep an eye open for things coming loose or going out of adjustment. But don't let that put you off – these are simple machines to maintain.

Kickstarting
Don't let the prospect of kickstarting put you off, either, because the small Triumph twins are very easy starters, especially if electronic ignition is fitted.

Usability
Triumphs are easy and very satisfying to ride on an open, twisty road, and there's nothing intimidating about these. But keep off motorways!

Parts availability
Excellent, with plenty of specialists and some new parts still being made. The exception is much of the tinwork, such as the infamous bathtub rear enclosure.

Parts costs
Reasonable – they actually cost less than some parts for modern bikes, but don't expect them to be much cheaper than those for the 650/750 Triumphs.

Insurance group
Go for a classic bike limited mileage policy, such as that offered by Carole Nash or Footman James, and you won't pay much for insurance, either.

Investment potential
None of the 350/500 twins has the ultimate glamour of big brother Bonneville, but collectors have caught on to their desirability, so prices have risen. They are unlikely to rise significantly now, but these bikes will keep their value.

Foibles
Triumph twins vibrate and leak oil – that's part of motorcycling folklore. However, the smaller 350/500 twins aren't as vibey as the bigger ones, and a well assembled engine in good condition shouldn't leak.

Plus points
Postwar Triumph twins are some of the most iconic motorcycles of all time, with good looks and torquey, punchy performance. Lightweight, too, if you're used to heavier modern bikes.

Minus points
Like any motorcycle of this era, the small Triumph twins need looking after, though they're no more fussy than any contemporary bike. They aren't as easy to find as the bigger Triumphs, and are slightly more expensive than the equivalent BSA, Matchless etc.

Alternatives
The only direct equivalent to the 350cc twin is the Norton Navigator, as almost all other British 350s of the 1950s/60s are singles. Alternatives to the 500 include the BSA A50, AJS Model 20 and Matchless G9, all of which are bigger and heavier than the Triumph; being scaled-down 650s rather than scaled-up 350s.

A shiny Tiger 100 is certainly the bike for this gentleman.

2 Cost considerations
– affordable, or a money pit?

Triumph spares, by and large, are not expensive. It's labour costs that mount up, rather than parts. If you are prepared to service the bike yourself, a small Triumph twin should be quite affordable to run, with 60-70mpg typical from the single-carb bikes. The prices quoted here are from a Triumph specialist and exclude local taxes.

Complete restoration (basket case to concours) around x10,000
Air cleaner (with chrome cover) x24
Alternator (Lucas RM19, stator only) x118
Brake shoes (rear) x29
Brake shoes (front, 7in) x27
Battery (12v) x27
Cam followers x36
Carburettor (Amal Concentric) x98
Clutch chainwheel x48
Clutch springs (3) x3.75
Cylinder barrel (500) x269
Downpipes x102pr
Electronic ignition x86
Fork stanchions x88 pair
Fork seals (external spring) x8.50

Gasket set x28
Gearbox sprocket x28
Headlamp shell x43
Mudguard (front) x55
Mudguard (rear) x125
Oil pump x65
Rear chain x50
Pistons (500) x135 pair
Primary chain x40
Rear shocks x101 pair
Seat x145
Silencers x200 pair
Speedometer (reconditioned) x260
Tank badge x49 each
Valves x17 each
Wiring loom x70

Many parts, such as carburettors, are still available new.

The C series Triumphs share a lot of parts.

3 Living with a Triumph twin
– will you get along together?

When new, Triumph C series twins had a good reputation as the perfect 'first big bike' for learners who had passed their test, and forsaken their BSA Bantam or Tiger Cub. And they deserved that reputation, as these are very easy machines to ride: lightweight, with good handling and peppy performance (except the 3TA).

All of this stands them in good stead today. If you're reading this book, you're probably not a novice rider, but all of those qualities that made the smaller Triumphs so popular through the 1960s are just as relevant today, and

A Tiger 100 makes a good all-rounder.

make them some of the easiest British classic bikes to live with.

However, if you've never owned a British classic before, don't let that user-friendly image fool you. These are still bikes from a different era that thrive on care and

Undeniably good looking, whatever the model.

As classics go, the smaller Triumph twins are quite easy to live with.

attention. Modern bikes often need only an oil check and chain adjustment between services, but classics need more hands-on ownership. This relationship is based on a constant awareness of how the bike is running: has that nut vibrated loose? Is that the beginnings of a leak from the rocker box? If an indicator ceases to function, is it the bulb or just a loose connector? Back in the '60s, keen young owners did use their Triumphs as everyday transport, but they also accepted the intensive maintenance that went with it.

Even today, some owners of the big Triumph twins do use them day-to-day, and it's possible to do so with the C series as well, though not if your commute includes fast main roads or motorways. These bikes are happy to cruise at 50-60mph, but ride them harder on a regular basis and bulbs will blow, oil leaks will develop, and bolt-on parts will come loose.

Having said all that, generally speaking, the later the model, the easier it is to live with, and there are some key upgrades – electronic ignition, oil filter and on earlier bikes the later front brake and 12-volt electrics – that can make any of these bikes less hassle day-to-day. Of course, a lot of owners would say that the extra attention an old Triumph (or any classic) needs is what makes owning one more satisfying than a modern bike. You develop a relationship with it that is quite different than with something that always starts on the button and never goes wrong. And although Triumph twins do need attention, they are basically simple and easy to maintain.

Although based around the same engine/gearbox unit (in 349cc or 490cc form), the C series twins came in a variety of guises. Really there are three basic types.

The original Twenty-one/3TA and 5TA were the tourers, built in a soft state of tune and with the famous 'bath tub' tinwork, though this was gradually lost over the years. A good choice for their period looks and easygoing natures.

Next up were the road bikes, which soon dropped the touring tinwork and came to be seen as mini versions of big brother Bonneville. There were 350 (Tiger 90) and 500 (Tiger 100) versions, both with a single carburettor. The ultimate sports road 500 was the Daytona, complete with twin carburettors and Bonneville E3134 profile cams. Fastest (and thirstiest) of the C series, the Daytona is slightly less easy to live with, having those two carbs to keep synchronised.

Finally, the C series had a long association with off-road competition, especially in the USA. Most of these off-road versions were exported to North America, though some have since been re-imported. All of them used the 500 engine in single-carb form, and are highly sought after now, especially the later high-pipe T100C.

The various incarnations of the C series encompassed a long production run, spanning 1957 to 1974. There were no drastic changes in that time, but there were some well worthwhile improvements. The main milestones were contact breaker ignition (1963/64), 12-volt electrics (1966), new frame ('67), improved fork damping ('68), timing side ball bearing with improved oil feed to the crank ('69) and improved engine breathing ('70).

Some of these changes can be applied to older machines, together with the aftermarket modifications (of which electronic ignition is key). Purists might protest about originality, but many of these changes hardly affect the bike's appearance. Whether you choose to change the bike or not is down to what sort of riding you're intending to do, how happy you are with fettling and whether you're a stickler for complete originality.

But even as standard, the Triumph C series twins make for lightweight, user-friendly bikes that will give anyone a lot of pleasure to ride and own.

4 Relative values

– which model for you?

See Chapter 12 for value assessment. This chapter shows, in relative percentage terms, the value of individual models in good condition. There were many variations on the C series theme over its long production life, and this chapter also looks at the strengths and weaknesses of each model, so that you can decide which is best for you. Basically, the various models can be divided into three types: tourers, road (single- and twin-carb) and competition/off-road.

Range availability

Tourers
1957-66 Twenty-one/3TA
1959-66 5TA Speed Twin

Road (single-carb)
1963-68 T90 Tiger 90
1960-61 T100A Tiger 100
1962-65 T100SS Tiger 100
1966 T100 Tiger 100
1967-70 T100S Tiger 100

Road (twin-carb)
1967-70 T100T Daytona
1971-74 T100R Daytona
1974 T100D Daytona Series 2

Competition/off-road
1961 TR5A/R & A/C
1962-65 T100S/R & S/C
1966-72 T100C
1973-74 TR5T Trophy Trail/Adventurer

1957-66 Tourers: 3TA & 5TA

The Twenty-one/3TA and 5TA C series are the softer end of the range, in a lower state of tune than the other bikes; very docile but still able to cruise at up to 60mph. The Twenty-one was the first of the line, launched in 1957 as an all-new 350cc twin.

Although it owed something to previous Triumphs it did incorporate several new features, notably unit construction of the engine and gearbox (the first unit Triumph twin) and voluminous tinwork. Designer Edward Turner aimed at a motorcycle that was clean and fuss-free, something

This really is a 3TA, which, over the years, has lost all its tinwork.

that would appeal beyond enthusiasts to the man in the street. Hence the big rear end enclosure, nicknamed the 'bathtub' because it looked like an inverted bath, plus valanced front mudguard and headlight nacelle. These all helped keep the rider and bike clean, but fashion changed in the early '60s, as motorcycling shifted towards a youth and leisure market. The average teenager saw the bike's panelling as a heavy, frumpy horror, and ditched the lot as soon as they could. Now of course, this same tinwork is one of the chief attractions, and any bike still fitted with it will be worth more.

Styling apart, the 350 Triumph offered 18.5bhp, enough for a top speed of around 80mph, with a four-speed gearbox and seven-inch drum brakes that were adequate for the time, but need thinking about in today's faster, heavier traffic. Renamed the 3TA in 1959, there were no major changes in its nine-year production life, though in a bow to fashion the bathtub was slimmed down to a much smaller 'bikini' rear enclosure in 1964, and even that was lost in the final year of '66. Over 20,000 Twenty-ones and 3TAs were built. One rarity to look out for is the military spec 3TA built for the Dutch Army in 1967.

The 3TA was joined by a bigger equivalent in 1959, almost identical to the original, but with the engine bored out to 490cc. This was the 5TA Speed Twin, which resurrected a famous name and delivered significantly more power – 27bhp at 6500rpm. Since the 5TA weighed only 10lb more than its little brother, performance was far better, though it remained a docile and flexible machine that was a tourer at heart. Changes were few, as on the 3TA, though for 1964 both bikes ditched their distributor ignition for a twin set of contact breaker points in the timing case, and twin coils.

Strengths/weaknesses: Flexible, easygoing and economical, with unique styling and presence. 3TA is not quick, and brakes on both bikes aren't up to modern standards, ditto the 6-volt electrics. Many bikes have lost their distinctive tinwork.
100%

5TA Speed Twin in all its bathtub glory, complete with 'Roman helmet' front mudguard and the famous Triumph nacelle.

Drive side of the 5TA: a mild-mannered tourer.

1960-70 Road: Tiger 90 & Tiger 100
The single-carburettor road bikes – the 349cc Tiger 90 and 490cc Tiger 100 – were in some ways the backbone of the range. In a higher state of tune and (apart from early

T100s) without the bathtub tinwork, they offered a more sporting alternative to the 3TA/5TA, and the Tiger 100 sold well. Today, it's the easiest to find of the entire range.

The Tiger 90 was one of the rarer C series bikes, with 3538 built. It was launched in 1963, with the abbreviated bikini panelling (lost the following year) and a higher state of tune than the 3TA, having a 9:1 compression ratio and twin Lucas contact

breakers in the timing cover. Power was boosted to 27bhp at 7500rpm, which gave the 350 impressive performance, as long as it was revved, and a top speed of nearly 90mph. Always in the shadow of the better-selling Tiger 100, it was nonetheless a very enjoyable bike to ride. It received a modified frame in 1965, 12-volt electrics in '66, new frame in '67, and different forks in '68, its final year.

The first Tiger 100, the T100A, actually arrived in 1960, with 9:1 high compression pistons and different camshafts to give 32bhp at 7000rpm. It also used Lucas Energy Transfer ignition which powered the coils directly

Nice 1964 Tiger 90, the 350cc sportster with bikini panelling, siamesed pipes, and original all-over white.

from the alternator, enabling it to run without a battery, though in practice this delivered difficult starting. Oddly, despite the T100A's sportier nature, it kept the 5TA's bathtub bodywork and high bars, unwanted by youthful owners – Triumph had made the same mistake with the first Bonneville in 1959! These touring parts were dropped for the US market in 1961, with the classic naked style that would be Triumph's hallmark throughout the '60s. UK buyers had to wait another three years.

Power was increased to 34bhp in '62, when the bike was renamed T100SS and received the same updates as the Tiger 90 through the decade (details of these

changes are in chapter 17), while the T100 also received a new cylinder head and shuttle-valve fork damping in 1968. The following year, the crankshaft's timing side plain bearing was replaced with a ball-bearing, which greatly strengthened the bottom end and improved lubrication. When the old plain bearing was worn, oil pressure to the rest of the crankshaft dropped, soon resulting in damage to both big-ends and main bearings. This feature was shared by all the 500s that year. Also in 1969 the front brake was upgraded to a twin-leading shoe. Finally, in 1970, the T100, like all the 500s, received a better breathing system which relieved crankcase

T100SS was the mainstay of the range in the mid-1960s.

pressure via the primary chaincase, reducing the chance of oil leaks. Over 10,000 Tiger 100s (with variations) had been built by 1968.

Strengths/weaknesses: A good compromise between the touring 3TA/5TA and twin-carb Daytona. Enjoyable performance and excellent handling. 1969/70 Tiger 100s have worthwhile modifications.

100%

Late Tiger 100: the result of a decade's development, and a fine practical classic.

1967-74 Road: Daytona

The Daytona is the sportster of the C series range, and is by far the fastest and most powerful. Inspired by Triumph's victories in the iconic races at Daytona, Florida in 1966 and '67, the bike capitalised on that success by taking the name of North America's most famous bike racing venue. It wasn't just a marketing ploy either, because the Daytona owed something to the race bikes.

Its new frame was based on that of the racers, with a thicker top tube and steeper steering head angle of 62 degrees. A new cylinder head, again based on the race experience, had a shallower combustion chamber and bigger valves at a narrower angle. The camshafts were based on the Bonneville's E3134 profile and (the biggest source of bragging rights for coffee bar cowboys) there were twin Amal Monobloc carburettors. This added up to 39bhp at 7400rpm, enough for a top speed of 104mph and 0-60mph in 7.0sec. The Daytona was both lighter and faster than its rival Honda CB450 'Black Bomber', if not as reliable or oil-tight. And it was a success, with over 7000 built in the first two years alone.

For 1968, the carburettors were updated with Amal Concentrics (as were the single-carb 500s that year) and there was a bigger 8in front brake to cope with the performance. The following year saw the same bottom end improvements as the other 500s, while the camshafts were now nitrided for a longer life and the brake was uprated again, to an 8in twin-leading shoe item.

One of the first Daytonas, with marginal single-leading shoe front brake and 'Tiger 100' badge.

Pretty 1971 Daytona in US spec.

Engine breather improvements were shared with the Tiger 100 in 1970, and for '71 the Daytona had several detail changes, including flashing indicators. There were no other major changes until production ended in 1974. There were plans for a Series 2 Daytona for 1975, using several Bonneville parts, including the forks, front disc brake, conical rear drum and silencers. Twelve pre-production bikes were built, but the model never reached production.

Strengths/weaknesses: Excellent performance, best brakes ('68 on), fine handling. Engine more highly stressed, and two carburettors to keep in tune.
130%

1961-74 competition/off-road: TR5A, T100C, TR5T

The 'competition' and/or 'off-road' C series bikes weren't quite as focused as these tags suggest. Although there were a few spec changes to make them more suitable for off-road competition, all were road-legal, and more like dual-purpose on/off-road trail bikes. But they remain some of the most stylish Triumphs of all time, with a high-pipe glamour associated with Steve McQueen and American desert racing.

Mechanically, most are almost identical to the road-going Tiger 100, and all are single carburettor only, making them easy-riding, adaptable machines that are capable of gentle green laning. They were aimed (TR5T apart) at the USA market, though some have since been reimported to Britain.

The first were the TR5A/R and TR5A/C of 1961, both based on the T100A but without the bathtub tinwork, adopting what became the classic Triumph look of separate chrome headlight and gaitered forks. The first machines had Energy Transfer Ignition, but this was soon dropped, with conventional battery/coil ignition fitted from engine number H21122. The TR5A/C is one of the rarest C series models of all – fewer than 700 were built.

They were renamed the T100S/R Tiger Road Sports and T100S/C Enduro Trophy for 1962; the latter with off-road tyres and a smaller fuel tank. Both bikes had a bracing strut between the steering head and frame top tube, while in '63 the distributor was dropped in favour of cb points in the timing case; the exhaust pipes were siamesed high-level, and alloy mudguards replaced steel.

For 1966, the S/C was renamed T100C with a stronger frame and two high-level silencers (previously just one) added in '67, plus a heat shield the following year. For 1969, as well as the same stronger bottom end as other 500s, the T100C had the same 8in twin-leading shoe front brake as the Daytona (from XC07584), while a bigger 'chip basket' heat shield protected the pillion's legs as well as the rider's. For '71, the T100C gained the same indicators and new switchgear as the Daytona, plus stainless steel mudguards, with no major changes for '72.

In 1973, with Triumph and parent company

The timing side of the T100C looked bare, with both pipes on the drive side.

BSA struggling to survive, the T100C was replaced by the TR5T Trophy Trail. The engine was carried over the little change, but housed in a BSA frame used for the 250 and 500cc off-road singles. This was completely different to the Triumph frame, housing engine oil in the big top and down tubes, with a swingarm mounted on needle-roller bearings. Rear chain adjustment was by snail cam plates on the frame.

Altogether, the Trophy Trail looked more like a serious off-road bike than the T100C, with high level front mudguard, 21in front wheel, off-road tyres, small alloy fuel tank and lower gearing. Front forks were the Triumph/ BSA Ceriani type, without gaiters. Renamed the Adventurer for 1974 (and with red tank flashes replacing the previous year's yellow) the TR5T was short-lived; a victim of the industry's collapse that year.

Strengths/weaknesses: All the virtues and vices of the Tiger 100, with off-road looks and some off-road ability. BSA-framed TR5T has less street scrambler style but more off-road ability.
T100C: 100%
TR5T: 95%

Arguably the T100C's best side. It was turning into a street scrambler, though its roots were in competition.

The TR5T was a last-ditch attempt at a trail bike.

Cheney Triumphs

Scrambles star Eric Cheney turned to frame building in 1961 for BSAs initially, but from 1965 for Triumph twins as well. His frames were designed specifically for off-road competiton, lighter and stronger than the standard frames, using Reynolds 531 or T45 steel tubing. Apart from some early twin downtube frames, most were single downtube with the big top and downtubes carrying the engine oil.

Many of these frames were exported to the USA, and some Cheney-framed Triumphs do survive, as highly desirable bikes. If you find one with a verifiable competition history, so much the better. Not all of these frames had numbers, but Eric's son Simon still builds frames and is able to verify age and authenticity – he can repair frames and supply spares. For contact details, see page 55.
160%

Genuine Cheney Triumphs are rare finds.

5 Before you view
– be well informed

To avoid a wasted journey, and the disappointment of finding that the bike does not match your expectations, it will help if you're very clear about what questions you want to ask before you pick up the phone. Some of these points might appear basic, but when you're excited about the prospect of buying your dream classic, it's amazing how some of the most obvious things slip the mind ... Also check the current values of the model you are interested in the classic bike magazine classified ads.

Where is the bike?
Is it going to be worth travelling to the next county/state, or even across a border? A locally-advertised machine, although it may not sound very interesting, can add to your knowledge for very little effort, so make a visit – it might even be in better condition than expected.

Dealer or private sale
Establish early on if the bike is being sold by its owner or by a trader. A private owner should have all the history, so don't be afraid to ask detailed questions. A dealer may have more limited knowledge of the bike's history, but should have some documentation. A dealer may offer a warranty/guarantee (ask for a printed copy).

Cost of collection and delivery
A dealer may well be used to quoting for delivery. A private owner may agree to meet you halfway, but only agree to this after you have seen the bike at the vendor's address to validate the documents. Conversely, you could meet halfway and agree the sale, but insist on meeting at the vendor's address for the handover.

View – when and where
It is always preferable to view at the vendor's home or business premises. In the case of a private sale, the bike's documentation should tally with the vendor's name and address. Arrange to view only in daylight, and avoid a wet day – the vendor may be reluctant to let you take a test ride if it's wet.

Reason for sale
Do make it one of the first questions. Why is the bike being sold and how long has it been with the current owner? How many previous owners?

Condition
Ask for an honest appraisal of the bike's condition. Ask specifically about some of the check items described in Chapter 9.

All original specification
A completely original Triumph will be worth more than a modified one, but certain mods (oil filter, electronic ignition) also indicate a conscientious owner who has been actively riding/caring for the machine.

Matching data/legal ownership

Do frame, engine numbers and licence plate match the official registration document? Is the owner's name and address recorded in the official registration documents?

For those countries that require an annual test of roadworthiness, does the bike have a document showing it complies (an MOT certificate in the UK, which can be verified on 0845 600 5977)?

In the UK, bikes registered in 1973 or earlier are exempt from VED (Vehicle Excise Duty, better known as road tax). At the time of writing, this was due to be extended in 2015 to 1974, meaning all C series Triumphs will qualify.

Does the vendor own the bike outright? Money might be owed to a finance company or bank: the bike could even be stolen. Several organisations will supply the data on ownership, based on the bike's licence plate number, for a fee. Such companies can often also tell you whether the bike has been 'written-off' by an insurance company. In the UK these organisations can supply vehicle data:

HPI – 01722 422 422 – www.hpicheck.com
AA – 0870 600 0836 – www.theaa.com
RAC – 0870 533 3660 – www.rac.co.uk
Other countries will have similar organisations.

Unleaded fuel

Has the bike been modified to run on unleaded fuel?

Insurance

Check with your existing insurer before setting out – your current policy might not cover you if you do buy the bike and decide to ride it home.

How you can pay

A cheque/check will take several days to clear and the seller may prefer to sell to a cash buyer. However, a banker's draft (a cheque issued by a bank) is as good as cash, but safer, so contact your own bank and become familiar with the formalities that are necessary to obtain one. Paying by electronic transfer via internet banking is the quickest means of all.

Buying at auction?

If the intention is to buy at auction see Chapter 10 for further advice.

Professional vehicle check (mechanical examination)

There are often marque/model specialists who will undertake professional examination of a vehicle on your behalf. Owners clubs may be able to put you in touch with such specialists.

6 Inspection equipment

– these items will really help

This book
Reading glasses (if you need them for close work)
Overalls
Camera
Compression tester
A friend, preferably a knowledgeable enthusiast

Before you rush out of the door, gather together a few items that will help as you work your way around the bike. This book is designed to be your guide at every step, so take it along and use the check boxes in chapter 9 to help you assess each area of the bike you're interested in. Don't be afraid to let the seller see you using it.

Take your reading glasses if you need them to read documents and make close-up inspections.

Be prepared to get dirty. Take along a pair of overalls, if you have them, and a camera, so that later you can study some areas of the bike more closely. Take a picture of any part of the bike that causes you concern, and seek a friend's opinion.

A compression tester is easy to use. It screws into the sparkplug holes, and on a Triumph twin these couldn't be easier to get to. With the ignition off, both sparkplugs out, turn the engine over on full throttle to get the compression reading.

Ideally, have a friend or knowledgeable enthusiast accompany you: a second opinion is always valuable.

7 Fifteen minute evaluation
– walk away or stay?

Engine/frame numbers

Engine and frame numbers are mentioned several times in this book, with good reason. They are unique to the bike, and a good means of checking several things: what year the bike left the factory; what model it is; whether the documentation actually relates to the bike, and whether the engine and frame are original.

The engine number is located on the drive side (left-hand side) of the crankcase, just below the cylinder barrel. Numbers should be clear: any 'fuzzy' numbers could be a sign of tampering.

Now look for the frame number, on the left-hand side of the headstock. This should carry the same number as the engine, and, if it doesn't, the bike has had a different engine fitted at some point. There may have been a good reason for this, but non-matching engine/ frame numbers reduce the bike's value.

However, finding non-matching numbers doesn't necessarily mean it's time to walk away. The bike itself may still be an honest machine with plenty to offer – you just need to make it clear to the seller that you know it isn't 100% original, and start negotiating on price.

The engine number is located on the drive side, just under the cylinder barrel.

Documentation

In the UK, the registration document is the V5C, which lists the name and address of the bike's registered keeper. This isn't necessarily the legal owner (though it usually is), but in any case, it should be the person selling the bike. If any explanations of differing details don't ring true (eg "I am selling it for a friend,") then walk away. Also check that the engine/frame numbers on the V5C are the same as those on the bike.

An annual roadworthiness certificate – the 'MoT' in the UK – is handy proof that the bike was roadworthy when tested, and if there's a whole sheaf of them gives evidence of the bike's history – when it was actively being used, and what the mileage was. The more of these that come with the bike, the better. Bikes built before 1960 no longer require an MoT in the UK.

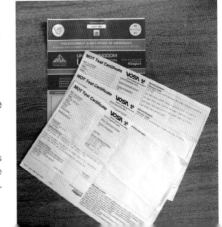

In the UK check the V5C, and previous MoT certificates – the more of these, the better.

General condition

Put the bike on its centre stand, to shed equal light on both sides, and take a good, slow walk around it. If it's claimed to be restored, and has a nice shiny tank and engine cases, look more closely – how far does the 'restored' finish go? Are the nooks and crannies behind the gearbox as spotless as the fuel tank? If not, the bike may have been given a quick smarten-up to sell. A generally faded look all over isn't necessarily a bad thing – it suggests a machine that hasn't been restored, and isn't trying to pretend that it has.

Now look at the engine – by far the most expensive and time-consuming thing to put right if anything's wrong. A lot of people will have told you that all old Triumphs leak oil, but there shouldn't be any serious leaks if the engine is in good condition and has been put together well. It shouldn't be spattered with lube, or have oily drips underneath. Even if it's dry on top, get down on your knees and have a peek at the underside of the crankcase – nice and dry, or covered in oil? A light misting here and there is nothing to worry about.

Take the bike off the centre stand and start the engine – it should fire up within two or three kicks, and rev up crisply and cleanly without showing blue or black smoke. Some top end clatter is normal, but listen for rumbles and knocks from the bottom end, and clonks from the primary drive – any of these are the precursors to serious work. While the engine's running, check that the ignition light or ammeter show the electrics are charging, and that the oil light (1969 on) goes out.

Switch the engine off and put the bike back on its centre stand. Check for play in the forks, headstock and swingarm. Are there leaks from the front forks or rear shocks? Are details like the seat, badges and tank colour right for the year of the bike? (A little research helps here, and the reference books listed at the end of this volume have all this information).

With the bike on its centre stand, have a good look around before starting it.

Are the bolt or screw heads chewed or rounded-off? Is there damage to casings around bolt heads? Has someone attacked fixings with a hammer and chisel? All are sure signs of a careless previous owner with more enthusiasm than skill, coupled with a dash of impatience. Not a good sign.

Are the engine and frame numbers correct for the year of the bike? Do they confirm that it's a genuine T100SS or Daytona? ('T100T' indicates this is a genuine Daytona). If not, you may still be looking at a completely usable bike, but it won't be worth as much as a genuine machine.

Listen to the engine running. Clonks or rumbles from the bottom end indicate the main or big-end bearings are worn. Excessive blue smoke will mean a worn top-end.

Minor oil leaks aren't a serious problem (though they are a bargaining point), but serious leaks suggest mechanical problems, and/or neglect. This is actually a 650cc Triumph, but the point is the same.

The frame number is at the top of the frame downtube, on the left-hand side. A repainted frame may make it difficult to decipher!

9 Serious evaluation
– 30 minutes for years of enjoyment

Circle the Excellent, Good, Average or Poor box of each section as you go along. The totting up procedure is detailed at the end of the chapter. Be realistic in your marking!

Engine/frame numbers

Engine and frame numbers should be the first thing you look at – they'll tell you whether the bike really is the model it's advertised as, and whether the engine (or frame) is the original one. Many Triumphs are advertised with 'matching numbers,' because the engine and frame numbers are the same, and therefore left the factory together.

The engine number is stamped on the left-hand side, just below the cylinder barrel: easy to find and to read. The figures should be clear and not 'fuzzy' – if they aren't, the number could have been tampered with, in which case walk away. From 1969 the engine number was stamped onto a background of Triumph logos, making

4️⃣ 3️⃣ 2️⃣ 1️⃣

Nice, clear, unadulterated engine number for a 3TA, 1963 model year. 'W' refers to radio equipment, so probably an ex-police bike.

From 1969 Triumph logos were stamped on to make tampering more difficult. This could be a later replacement crankcase, as no engine number is visible.

The frame number should match the engine number.

tampering more difficult. The model code ('T90', 'T100' etc) will be stamped to the left of the number, so check that this agrees with the seller's description – model codes, with their production years, are listed in Chapter 17.

Now look for the frame number, stamped on the left-hand side of the headstock. This may be more difficult to read, especially if the frame has been repainted or powder coated, but it should still be visible. All the same comments apply. It's worth noting that if the frame and engine numbers don't match, the bike may still be honest and usable, but being non-original should be reflected in the price.

Finally, check that these numbers match those on the registration document. If they don't, then it really is time to walk away.

Paint

Triumphs have always been good-looking bikes, and the paintwork makes a big contribution to this. The good news is that (unless you're looking at a bathtub Twenty-one, 3TA or 5TA) there's not that much of it, just tank, side panels and mudguards – all T100Cs have alloy or stainless steel guards, making a repaint simpler still. Having said that, don't underestimate the cost of a professional paint job, which is well worth having done, as the fuel tank in particular is such a focal point of the bike.

Look for evidence of quick and cheap resprays, with pinstriping, for example, that doesn't line up with the tank badges. Light staining around the filler cap, from spilt fuel, should polish out, but might require a respray. Generally, faded original paintwork isn't necessarily a bad thing, and in fact some riders prefer this unrestored look – there are so many restored Triumphs around, that an honest-looking original, even if a little faded around the edges, has its own appeal.

Many C series Triumphs had some sort of two-tone colour scheme, and for originality it's important to get the right one for the year of the bike, along with its correct pinstriping. The reference books give a complete listing. Paint availability shouldn't be a problem, as there are often modern equivalents – Triumph Riveria Blue from the '60s, for example (used on the Tiger 90 for 1968), is the same as Ford metallic blue.

Original paintwork in good condition is the best find.

Beautiful two-tone scallops really set off a tank.

Chrome

Chrome plating is another big visual plus on these Triumphs, used on the silencers, headlamp shell, handlebars, parcel grid, mirrors and some mudguards, tank badges, and other parts. The quality of Meriden's original plating is generally pretty good, though we are talking at least 30 years on now, so don't expect any original brightwork to be pristine.

Whichever bike you're looking at, check the chrome for rust, pitting and general dullness. Minor blemishes can be polished away, but otherwise you're looking at a replating bill. If the silencers are seriously rotted, it's a better idea to budget for a new pair – less hassle than getting the old ones replated, in any case.

A shiny parcel grid is a distinctive Triumph feature.

Poor chrome (which this isn't, of course), is not a reason to reject a bike, but a good bargaining lever.

Tinwork

In one respect, buying a secondhand bike is far easier than purchasing a used car – there's far less bodywork to worry about. Of course, that's not so true of the Twenty-one, 3TA, 5TA and early T100A, with their bathtub enclosure, headlight nacelle and valanced front mudguard. If these have survived, check for rust and dents. New front mudguards in most styles are available, and old-stock nacelles do come up. At the time of writing, bathtubs and bikinis are not available new.

Check mudguards for straightness.

Mudguards should be straight, free of rust around the rims and securely bolted to the bike. Apart from the high-level front guard of the TR5T, all are substantial items with two or three stays.

Apart from those with bathtub or bikini enclosures (and the TR5T), all bikes had rounded gloss black side panels, the right-hand one acting as an oil tank, and the matching left-hand one housing the toolkit, though US bikes didn't receive this left-hand panel until 1967. The oil tank should be checked for leaks through the seams, as repair entails removal and flushing out before it can be put right.

The fuel tank needs to be checked for leaks around the tap and along the seams, as well as dents and rust. Watch out for patches of filler. As with the oil tank, repairing leaks means flushing it out (which has to be thorough – you don't want any petrol vapour hanging about when the welding torch

The bathtub should be dent-free.

Many bikes have lost their nacelles, which is a nice period feature.

Not many bikini panels have survived.

is fired up) but the fuel tank is at least easier to remove. Pinhole leaks can often be cured by Petseal, but anything more serious needs a full repair. If the tank is beyond saving, new ones are available, though make sure to get the right one for your bike – there are six different types. The new tank might also need painting, but either way this isn't a cheap option, making a very poor condition tank a good bargaining lever.

Seat

Whichever seat the bike has, the points to look for are the same. The metal pan can rust, which will eventually give way, though this is easy to check. Covers can split, which of course allows rain in, which the foam padding soaks up … and never dries out. That's a recipe for a permanently wet backside, or a rock hard seat on frosty mornings (the author speaks from experience). New covers and complete seats in various styles are available, though recovering an old seat is a specialist job. The 1957/58 Twenty-one had a very neat underseat rubber tooltray, with cutouts to accommodate each tool. It tends to collect water, but is a lovely period piece if it's survived.

Slightly grubby 1968 seat – grey top is original.

Late seats had a 'perforated' top.

Check seat for splits and tears. This the ¾-length TR5T item.

Footrest/kickstart rubbers

Worn footrest rubbers are a good sign of high mileage, though as they're so cheap and easy to replace, not an infallible one. They should be secure on the footrest and free of splits or tears. If the footrest itself is bent upwards, that's a sure sign the bike has been down the road at some point, so look for other telltale signs on that side. The kickstart and gearchange rubbers are also easy to replace, so well worn ones could indicate owner neglect. On kickstart bikes, beware the worn smooth rubber on the kickstart lever – your foot's liable to slip off when using it, with painful results

Split footrest rubbers will need replacing   Used, but intact, footrest rubber.

as the kickstart lever slams back into your leg. The rubber should also be firm on the lever and not drop off after half a dozen kicks. Of course, if the engine needs that many kicks to fire it up, then something's wrong there anyway.

Frame

4 3 2 1

All C series Triumphs except the TR5T use a variation on the same basic tubular steel frame with a single downtube. This was adequate for the Twenty-one/3TA, but the unsupported headstock could lead to vague steering, which became more serious as the 500s came on stream.

Triumph added a bolt-on reinforcing strut to US competition bikes for 1960, but didn't introduce a fully brazed strut across the range until the 1966 model year, reducing the steering head angle to 65 degrees at the same time. The result was stiffer, but still not good enough, so a final version of the frame arrived for '67, with a thicker support strut, strong mounting plates for the swingarm pivot and an even steeper steering head of 62 degrees. Partly developed from racing experience at Daytona, this did the trick, and was used until 1974.

The TR5T is the exception, using a version of the BSA singles frame, which was all-welded with engine oil in the top tube and the swingarm supported by needle-roller bearings.

Whichever frame the bike has, the most important job is to check if it is straight and true. Crash damage may have bent it, putting the wheels out of line. One way of checking is by an experienced eye, string, and a straight

The downtube is the most accessible part of the frame.

A frame in this condition needs a complete strip down and repaint – unless you can live with it.

Check any brackets as well.

edge, but the surest way to ascertain a frame's straightness is on the test ride – any serious misalignment should be obvious in the way the bike handles.

A really shabby frame necessitates a strip down and repaint, though as with the other paintwork, if it's original and fits in with the patina of the bike, then there's a good case for leaving it as it is.

Look for bent brackets, which can be heated and bent back into shape, and cracks around them, which can be welded. Those for horn and exhaust pipes are usually the first to succumb to vibration.

Stands

All bikes were fitted with a side stands, and most have a centre stand as well, though some owners remove these to improve corning clearance.

Both stands should be secure. When on the centre stand, the bike shouldn't wobble or lean – a sign of serious stand wear and/or imminent collapse. This affects bikes which have been started and left idling on the centre stand – all the vibration is transmitted to ground via the stand, which doesn't do it much good.

Side and centre stands should be wobble-free.

Lights

Triumph electrics improved dramatically with the 12-volt system in 1966, which will support a halogen headlight bulb. Whatever the age, look for a tarnished or rusted reflector, which is an MOT failure, though reflectors, bulbs, glass and headlight shells are all available. The same style of rear light was fitted to everything until 1967, when the T100C and US models received a new type with separate reflector and rear/stop light. A big squared-off rear light was

Late rear light, with separate light and reflector.

A halogen bulb will give the headlight a boost.

fitted for 1973. These should all be available as pattern parts, though one handy modification that doesn't alter the outward appearance in any way is an LED rear light bulb. This is a straight swap for the standard bulb, but won't blow, leaving you taillight-less on a dark night. Bikes with small side reflectors front and rear are likely to be US models.

Electrics/wiring

Triumph electrics don't have the best reputation, but the 12-volt zener diode system from 1966 is pretty good, and all bikes can be significantly improved with aftermarket items. Early Twenty-one, 3TAs and 5TAs used a car-type distributor, which is prone to wear, and thus to erratic ignition timing. The Energy Transfer ignition on early T100As and US exports proved troublesome in practice and was soon dropped. The distributor was replaced by twin contact breaker points in the timing cover and twin coils on the Tiger 90/100 in 1963, which still wasn't ideal, but Lucas 6CA cb points from 1968 allowed each cylinder to be timing separately, which was the best factory system.

The zener diode gets rid of excess charge on the 1966-on 12-volt bikes.

What do the connectors and wiring look like? Nice and neat?

Alternators are generally reliable.

An intermittent rear brakelight could be down to corrosion in the switch (mounted on the chainguard).

The ultimate answer to all of this is electronic ignition, and if an owner has fitted that, so much the better. Electrex World now offers a compact ignition/lighting system that replaces the alternator, coils, cb points and (if fitted) distributor in one fell swoop.

Even if it's had these later sensible modifications, the electrical system still needs checking. A good general indication of the owner's attitude is the condition of the wiring – is it tidy and neat, or flopping around? The many bullet connectors need to be clean and tight, and many odd electrical problems are simply down to bad connections or a poor earth. Up to 1970, most bikes came with an ammeter, which at least gives some indication that all is well in the charging circuit. Early 'ignition' warning lights are there simply to inform you that the ignition is on, not whether the alternator is doing its job.

Finally, check that everything works: lights, horn, indicators (fitted post '71, but sometimes removed by owners) and stop light (water can enter the rear brake switch).

Wheels/tyres

4 3 2 1

All of these bikes used spoked wheels with chromed steel rims. Check the chrome condition on the rims – rechroming entails a complete dismantle and rebuild of the wheel – and that the rim is straight. It's easy to spin the wheel and check for straightness while the bike's on its centre stand, but if it doesn't have one you'll need a strong helper to balance the bike on the sidestand to get each wheel clear of the ground first. Check that none of the spokes are loose and give each one a gentle tap with a screwdriver – any that are 'offkey' will need retensioning. Ask if the bike has a QD (quickly detachable) rear wheel, which was an option. This was a handy feature that mounted the wheel on splines, allowing it to be removed without disturbing the chain or rear brake.

Check spokes are all there and sound.

Tyres are easy to check.

A modern tyre that you wouldn't find on a classic Triumph, but anything in this condition needs immediate replacement!

Tyres should have at least the legal minimum of tread. That's at least 1mm of tread depth across at least three-quarters of the breadth of the tyre. If the tread doesn't reach that far across the breadth (true of some modern tyres) then any tread showing must be at least 1mm deep. Beware of bikes that have been left standing (especially on the sidestand) for some time, allowing the tyres to crack and deteriorate – it's no reason to reject the bike, but a good lever to reduce the price. New tyres in suitable sizes are no problem at all.

Wheel bearings

4️⃣ 3️⃣ 2️⃣ 1️⃣

Wheel bearings aren't expensive, but fitting them is a hassle, and if there's play it could affect the handling. To check them, put the bike on its centre stand, put the steering on full lock and try rocking the front wheel in a vertical plane, then spin the wheel and listen for signs of roughness. Do the same for the rear wheel. If they do need replacing, try to find sealed replacements, which will last longer.

Checking the rear wheel bearings for play.

Steering head bearings

4️⃣ 3️⃣ 2️⃣ 1️⃣

Again, the bearings don't cost an arm or leg, but trouble here can affect the handling, and changing them is a big job. With the bike on the centre stand (or balanced on the sidestand) swing the handlebars from lock to lock. They should move freely, with not a hint of roughness or stiff patches – if there is, budget for replacing them. To check for play, take the bike off the stand, put the front brake on hard and attempt to rock the bike gently back and forth – any play should be obvious.

Steering head bearing check.

Try rocking the swingarm from side-to-side.

Swing arm bearings

4 3 2 1

Another essential for good handling is the swing arm bearings. These should have been regularly greased, and if they haven't, rapid wear or even seizure can result, the latter if the bike has been left standing for some time. To check for wear, get hold of the rear end of the arm on one side and try rocking the complete swing arm from side-to-side. There should be no perceptible movement. If there is, haggle on the price, as replacement is a difficult job.

Suspension

4 3 2 1

The forks were typical of the period, at first with internal springs, two-way damping and steel stanchions. From 1964 (on the T100SS) the forks were strengthened with external springs (still hidden by gaiters) and bigger oil seal carriers. Those on the TR5T were completely different, being the Ceriani type with alloy sliders, steel stanchions and no gaiters. All bikes had Girling type rear shocks, which were shrouded until 1969.

Checking for play in the forks. This may also highlight play in the steering head bearings.

Check shocks for leaks. Pre-'69 shocks were shrouded.

Gaiters should be free of splits and tears.

Check both forks and rear shocks for leaks. The fork stanchions' chrome plate eventually pits, especially when exposed to the elements and/or the bike has been used in winter. When that happens, it rapidly destroys the oil seals – hence the leaks. New stanchions, or reground and replated existing ones, are the answer, as there's little point in fitting new seals to rough forks. The shocks are easy to check for leaks, but if the forks have gaiters, try rubbing the gaiter against the stanchion inside it. If it moves very easily, then there's likely to be a leak.

Check for play by grabbing the bottom of the forks and trying to rock them back and forth; play here indicates worn bushes. Worn out rear shocks will manifest themselves as a high speed weave, and sick forks will likewise spoil the bike's handling.

Instruments

Instrumentation on earlier bikes was the British period standard of speedometer and ammeter, a rev counter being first optional, then standard on the road bikes.

There were various styles, depending on year, but Triumph instruments didn't change as frequently as the rest of the bike, with grey-faced matching Smiths speed and rev counter replaced by black-faced ones in 1971. Don't expect the ammeter to give a foolproof reading at high revs, but so long as it shows a positive charge with the lights on at moderate revs, all is well.

Checking the speedo works obviously has to wait for the test ride – if nothing is working, the cable is the most likely culprit, but if either mileometer or speedo have ceased to function while the other is still working, then there's something wrong internally. Instrument repair is best left to a specialist – a battered and bent chrome bezel suggests that a previous

Nacelle-mounted speedo and ammeter on a 5TA.

owner has had a go themselves. The speedo drive gearbox is mounted on the rear wheel, but it's more usually the cable at fault than the box.

Grey-faced rev counter and speedo from 1967.

The speedo drive gearbox is mounted on the rear wheel.

Engine/gearbox – general impression

You can tell a lot about the likely condition of a Triumph twin without hearing it run. These engines are easy to work on, and the drawback is that it encourages keen and/or impecunious

This late Daytona hasn't run for some time, but it looks all-there and unbutchered.

owners to take things apart themselves, often without the proper tools or knowledge. Look for chewed up screw or allen bolt heads and rounded off bolts, plus damage to the casings surrounding them. Tappet covers can come loose and fly off if not properly secured, so check the retaining clips (fitted from 1963) are in contact with the caps.

They don't have to leak!

It's part of motorcycling folklore that old Triumphs leak oil, but it's not necessarily the case. As long as the engine is in good condition and has been properly put together, it should be reasonably oil tight. But still, look for leaks at the barrel/crankcase joint, around the pushrod tubes and the underside of the crankcase. Some light misting isn't a bad sign, but if the bike has a puddle of oil underneath it, and the engine/gearbox is covered in lubricant, then walk away – unless, of course, the price reflects the condition. An engine like that is likely to need a complete rebuild, though Triumph engines will keep running when in poor condition.

This one's leaking between the barrel and crankcase.

Many of the same comments apply to the gearbox – look for chewed fasteners and signs of neglect. Remove the oil filler cap and stick a finger inside to check whether the oil has been changed recently – nice clean EP90 … or a frothy sludge.

Quiz the owner about engine modifications: cartridge oil filter, electronic ignition, Morgo oil pump and allen-head tappet adjusters are all good signs.

Do the tappet covers have their clips in place? These do.

Engine – starting/idling

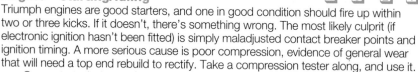

Triumph engines are good starters, and one in good condition should fire up within two or three kicks. If it doesn't, there's something wrong. The most likely culprit (if electronic ignition hasn't been fitted) is simply maladjusted contact breaker points and ignition timing. A more serious cause is poor compression, evidence of general wear that will need a top end rebuild to rectify. Take a compression tester along, and use it.

Once started, the engine should idle evenly on both cylinders. If it sounds and feels lumpy and uneven, then contact breaker or carburettor adjustments are the most likely cause, but a knowledgeable owner should already have these spot-on. If the carburettor is worn, both new parts and complete carbs are available. Another possible cause of uneven idling and running is damage to the hoses connecting the carburettor to the air filter and inlet stub – this can cause air leaks and upset the mixture.

Kickstarting isn't difficult, and the engine should fire up readily ...

... and idle evenly without lumpiness.

Engine – smoke/noise

If you're used to quiet, modern water-cooled engines, don't be alarmed by the merry clattering emanating from the Triumph's rocker boxes, as they all do that. Even among old British bikes, the Triumph twin had a reputation for mechanical noise from the top end. Adjusting the tappets is an easy enough job, though access is easier on the final bikes, which have an access hole for feeler gauges.

Blue smoke means the cylinders, pistons/rings, valves or guides are worn. This is a '77 Bonneville, but blue smoke from an older bike looks the same!

A sign of real trouble is knocking or rumbling from the bottom end, which will mean a complete engine rebuild for sure. Whether it's big-ends or mains that need attention, the cure entails taking the engine out and completely stripping it. Don't buy a bike that's making these noises unless it's cheap. Engine parts to cure all of this are no problem at all, for all bikes. 1969-on bikes, with their ball-race timing side main bearing and crank-end oil feed (giving a more consistent supply of lube) are less prone to bottom end problems.

While the engine is idling, hinge up the seat, remove the oil tank cap, and take a peek inside – you should see a spurt of oil being returned to the tank, which increases with revs. If there's nothing, switch off immediately, as this means the oil pump isn't scavenging, and damage could ensue. This is usually down to the ball-valve in the pump not seating properly, and is relatively simple to put right, but the bike can't be run until it is.

Refit the tank cap, then look back at the silencers and blip the throttle. Blue smoke means the engine is burning oil and is a sign of general wear in the top end, which isn't unusual. That usually means a rebore. Again, parts are available, including oversize pistons, though standard size barrels less so. Inevitably, other problems will come up once the engine is apart, as the valves and guides will probably need replacing as well. Guides can also come loose in the head, but that won't be obvious until the top end has been taken apart.

With the engine running, check that oil is returning to the tank.

Black smoke, indicating rich running, is less of a problem, caused by carburettor wear, or (fingers crossed) simply a blocked air filter. Bikes without air filters should be avoided, as you don't know what nasties the motor has ingested.

Primary drive

The C series clutch is generally reliable, and problems come from general wear rather than any fundamental weakness. Listen to the primary drive while the engine is running. Noises from this area – clonks or rumbles – could be caused by one of a number of things. It could be wear in the clutch and its shock absorber, the engine sprocket chattering on worn splines or the alternator rotor coming loose on the crank's driving shaft. Of course, you won't know which without taking off the primary drive cover, but if the seller acknowledges that a noise is there, it's another good lever to reduce the price.

Liston for rumbles from the primary drive. 1968-on primary covers have an access plate bearing the Triumph logo.

In theory, the primary chain, running in its nice, clean oil bath, should have long life, but even here an eye needs to be kept on it. Adjustment of the chain tensioner (fitted from 1960) through the drain plug hole, is messy and awkward – it's easier with the proper tool, but may have been neglected.

Chain/sprockets

With the engine switched off, examine the final drive chain and sprockets. Is the chain clean, well lubed and properly adjusted? The best way to check how worn it is is to take hold of a link on the sprocket and try to pull it rearwards, away from the sprocket. It should only reveal a small portion of the sprocket teeth – any more, and it needs replacing.

Check the rear sprocket teeth for wear – if they have a hooked appearance, the sprocket needs replacing. Ditto if any teeth are damaged or missing. And if the rear sprocket needs replacing, then the gearbox sprocket will, too. Chain and sprockets aren't massively expensive, but changing the gearbox sprocket takes some dismantling time.

Chains don't wear quickly, but still need looking after.

Battery

Lift up the seat and check the battery (or in the case of early 12-volt bikes, twin 6-volt batteries). Acid splashes indicate overcharging. The correct electrolyte level is a good sign of a meticulous owner; do check that the battery is

This battery is missing its retaining strap.

securely held in place by its rubber strap. If it isn't, the battery can leap upwards over bumps and short out against the metal seat base. (Again, author's experience.)

Engine/gearbox mountings

These need to be completely solid, with no cracks, and no missing or loose bolts – if not, the bike is not in a rideable condition. The exact design changed over the years (some were welded to the frame, some bolted) but the points to check are the same.

Check engine mountings and bolts – this is perfect.

Exhaust

Exhaust systems may be two-into-two low level pipes on road bikes, or two-into-two (or one) high-level for off-roaders. Some (low or high level) have since been fitted to two-into-one systems because they save a bit of weight and look cool. The T100C's high level system probably takes the prize for appearance.

Check that the downpipes are secure in the cylinder head (looseness causes air leaks) and examine all joints for looseness and leaks, all of which are MoT failures. The silencers should be secure, firmly mounted and in solid condition. Replacements for the various types are all available.

Pipes are very accessible and easy to check.

Test ride

The test ride should be not less than 15 minutes, and you should be doing the riding – not the seller riding with you on the pillion. It's understandable that some sellers are reluctant to let a complete stranger loose on their pride and joy, but it does go with the territory of selling a bike, and so long as you leave an article of faith (usually the vehicle you arrived in) then a test ride is a reasonable request. Take your driving licence in case the seller wants to see it.

Main warning lights

4 3 2 1

All bikes have an ignition warning light, but this only serves to tell you that the ignition is on – it doesn't warn of poor charging, which is what the ammeter is for. An oil pressure warning light was fitted to the Daytona from mid-1968, though this isn't infallible.

Pre-1968 bikes have just ignition and main beam warning lights.

Engine performance

4 3 2 1

A Triumph twin in good condition should give good acceleration in the mid-range. The low powered Twenty-one/3TA will seem slow, but all bikes should pull cleanly. And despite all the talk of vibration, these engines are reasonably smooth and free-revving up to 4000rpm. The Daytona will happily rev far higher, though vibes start to come in.

Check for hesitation, which shouldn't happen – a bike with well set-up ignition and carburetion will pull crisp and clean. Spitting back through the

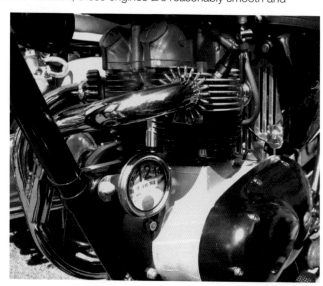

Looks good, and the engine shouldn't feel flat and lifeless, either.

carb can be caused by the absence of an air filter, and the bike should be quite tractable at low speeds, without jerks or hesitation.

If possible, cruise the bike at 55-60mph for five minutes, then check for oil leaks – there shouldn't be anything more than a slight misting. A typical comfortable cruising speed is around 50-60mph for the Twenty-one/3TA, slightly more for the Tiger 90 and 60-70mph for the 500s.

All engines should pull happily from low revs with no hesitation.

Clutch operation

The clutch is heavier than on some modern bikes, but take up should be smooth and positive. Nor should it drag or slip, despite the tales of all Triumph clutches dragging. To check this, select first gear from a standstill. A small crunch is normal, but a full-blooded graunch, followed by a leap forward, means the clutch is dragging. However, the cure is usually down to careful adjustment rather than the wholesale replacement of parts.

Gearbox operation

Triumph gearboxes work well, with a clean, positive shift. Watch for stiffness, notchiness and whining. They're also reliable, and given regular oil changes should not give trouble. Difficulty in finding neutral at a standstill is not inevitable, so long as the clutch has been set up correctly, so reluctance here is no reason to suspect the bike, though it's often easier to slip into neutral just as you roll to a standstill. However, false neutrals, or slipping out of gear, are sure signs of trouble.

Handling

Triumph's reputation for making good handling bikes, especially from the mid-1960s onwards, was well deserved, and the same holds true today. Bear in mind though that early bikes are not as surefooted at high speeds as the later machines.

These are relatively light bikes with stiff suspension, very agile and easy to flick through corners. So any vagueness and weaving is usually down to worn forks, rear shocks or tyres – it's not inherent. They should never feel soft and wallowy – if they do, the suspension condition is your first thing to recheck. If the bike pulls to one side in a straight line, the wheels may be out of line.

Brakes

All the C series Triumphs (except a small final batch of Daytona T100Ds) used cable-operated drum brakes, which were adequate when new, but need taking into account when riding in fast, heavy traffic. Up to 1968, all used the same 7in single-leading shoe front drum, with a similar brake at the rear. Adequate for the Twenty-one/3TA, they were questionable for the higher powered 500s. Adjusted properly, these brakes are good enough, but their limitations still need bearing in mind.

In 1968, the Daytona received an 8in front drum, and was upgraded again in '69 to the twin-leading shoe 8in brake from the 650cc Triumphs. The latter is widely regarded as one of Triumph's best brakes ever, and is a good retro fit to other C series bikes – the author's Tiger 90 was one such. The same year, 1969, saw the T100S and T100C given a 7in version of this brake.

The TR5T, with its off-road bias, had smaller brakes (6in front and 7in rear) in conical hubs – they're fine for green laning, but a retrograde step for modern roads.

On the test ride, don't expect modern power from any of these, but all of them work well enough. The lever should not feel spongey, shouldn't 'pulse' (the sign of an out-of-round drum) or reach close to the bars on a hard stop.

The 7-inch single-leading shoe brake fitted to most C series Triumphs isn't up to fast riding.

The 8-inch twin-leading shoe front brake from the bigger Triumphs is the best of the bunch, and can be retro-fitted – some already have been.

The 6-inch conical drum on the TR5T is fine off-road; not okay on Tarmac.

Cables

All the control cables – brakes, clutch, throttle and choke – should work smoothly without stiffness or jerking. Poorly lubricated, badly adjusted cables are an indication of general neglect, and the same goes for badly routed cables.

Stiff cables are a sign of neglect.

Switchgear

Switchgear varied according to year. Most had a combined horn/dip switch on the bars, and nacelle-equipped bikes had a rotary ignition/light switch neatly mounted in the nacelle. Later machines had these on the left-hand side panel, and later still a lighting toggle switch was fitted to the headlight shell. From 1971, all-new Lucas alloy switches were fitted to the bars, confusingly unlabelled and awkward to use.

Whatever is fitted, check that it works positively and reliably. Malfunctioning switches are usually a simple problem to solve, but another reason to bargain over price.

A combined horn/dipswitch is the most common fitment.

The 1971-73 Lucas switchgear is unlabelled.

Evaluation procedure

Add up the total points.

Score: 132 = excellent; 99 = good; 66 = average; 33 = poor. Bikes scoring over 92 will be completely usable and will require only maintenance and care to preserve condition. Bikes scoring between 33 and 67 will require some serious work (at much the same cost regardless of score). Bikes scoring between 68 and 91 will require very careful assessment of the necessary repair/restoration costs in order to arrive at a realistic value.

10 Auctions
– sold! Another way to buy your dream

Auction pros & cons

Pros: Prices will usually be lower than those of dealers or private sellers and you might grab a real bargain on the day. Auctioneers have usually established clear title with the seller. At the venue you can usually examine documentation relating to the bike.

Cons: You have to rely on a sketchy catalogue description of condition & history. The opportunity to inspect is limited and you cannot ride the bike. Auction machines can be a little below par and may require some work. It's easy to overbid. There will usually be a buyer's premium to pay in addition to the auction hammer price.

Which auction?

Auctions by established auctioneers are advertised in the motorcycle magazines and on the auction houses' websites. A catalogue, or a simple printed list of the lots for auctions might only be available a day or two ahead, though often lots are listed and pictured on auctioneers' websites much earlier. Contact the auction company to ask if previous auction selling prices are available as this is useful information (details of past sales are often available on websites).

Catalogue, entry fee and payment details

When you purchase the catalogue of the bikes in the auction, it often acts as a ticket allowing two people to attend the viewing days and the auction. Catalogue details tend to be comparatively brief, but will include information such as 'one owner from new, low mileage, full service history', etc. It will also usually show a guide price to give you some idea of what to expect to pay and will tell you what is charged as a 'Buyer's premium'. The catalogue will also contain details of acceptable forms of payment. At the fall of the hammer an immediate deposit is usually required, the balance payable within 24 hours. If the plan is to pay by cash there may be a cash limit. Some auctions will accept payment by debit card. Sometimes credit or charge cards are acceptable, but will often incur an extra charge. A bank draft or bank transfer will have to be arranged in advance with your own bank as well as with the auction house. No bike will be released before all payments are cleared. If delays occur in payment transfers then storage costs can accrue.

Buyer's premium

A buyer's premium will be added to the hammer price: don't forget this in your calculations. It is not usual for there to be a further state tax or local tax on the purchase price and/or on the buyer's premium.

Viewing

In some instances it's possible to view on the day or days before, as well as in the hours prior to, the auction. There are auction officials available who are willing to help out if need be. While the officials may start the engine for you, a test ride is out of the question. Crawling under and around the bike as much as you want is permitted. You can also ask to see any documentation available.

Bidding

Before you take part in the auction, decide your maximum bid - and stick to it!

It may take a while for the auctioneer to reach the lot you are interested in, so use that time to observe how other bidders behave. When it's the turn of your bike, attract the auctioneer's attention and make an early bid. The auctioneer will then look to you for a reaction every time another bid is made. Usually the bids will be in fixed increments until the bidding slows, when smaller increments will often be accepted before the hammer falls. If you want to withdraw from the bidding, make sure the auctioneer understands your intentions - a vigorous shake of the head when he or she looks to you for the next bid should do the trick!

Assuming that you are the successful bidder, the auctioneer will note your card or paddle number, and from that moment on you will be responsible for the bike.

If it is unsold, either because it failed to reach the reserve or because there was little interest, it may be possible to negotiate with the owner, via the auctioneers, after the sale is over.

Successful bid

There are two more items to think about - how to get the bike home, and insurance. If you can't ride it, your own or a hired trailer is one way, another is to have it shipped using the facilities of a local company. The auction house will also have details of companies specialising in the transport of bikes.

Insurance for immediate cover can usually be purchased on site, but it may be more cost-effective to make arrangements with your own insurance company in advance, and then call to confirm the full details.

eBay & other online auctions

eBay & other online auctions once had a reputation for bargains. You could still land a Triumph at a bargain price, though many traders as well as private sellers now use eBay and prices have risen. As with any auction, the final price depends how many buyers are bidding and how desperately they want the bike!

Either way, it would be foolhardy to bid without examining the bike first, which is something most vendors encourage. A useful feature of eBay is that the geographical location of the bike is shown, so you can narrow your choices to those within a realistic radius of home. Be prepared to be outbid in the last few moments of the auction. Remember, your bid is binding and that it will be very, very difficult to get restitution in the case of a crooked vendor fleecing you - caveat emptor! Look at the seller's rating as well as the bike.

Be aware that some bikes offered for sale in online auctions are 'ghost' machines. Don't part with any cash without being sure that the vehicle does actually exist and is as described (usually pre-bidding inspection is possible).

Auctioneers

Bonhams www.bonhams.com/ British Car Auctions (BCA) www.bca-europe.com or www.british-car-auctions.co.uk/ Cheffins www.cheffins.co.uk/ eBay www.eBay.com/ H&H www.classic-auctions.co.uk/ Shannons www.shannons.com.au/ Silver www.silverauctions.com

11 Paperwork

– correct documentation is essential!

The paper trail

Classic bikes sometimes come with a large portfolio of paperwork accumulated and passed on by a succession of proud owners. This documentation represents the real history of the machine, from which you can deduce how well it's been cared for, how much it's been used, which specialists have worked on it and the dates of major repairs and restorations. All of this information will be priceless to you as the new owner, so be very wary of bikes with little paperwork to support their claimed history.

Registration documents

All countries/states have some form of registration for private vehicles whether it's like the American 'pink slip' system or the British 'log book' system.

It is essential to check that the registration document is genuine, that it relates to the bike in question, and that all the details are correctly recorded, including frame and engine numbers (if these are shown). If you are buying from the previous owner, his or her name and address will be recorded in the document: this will not be the case if you are buying from a dealer.

In the UK the current (Euro-aligned) registration document is the V5C, and is printed in coloured sections of blue, green and pink. The blue section relates to the motorcycle specification, the green section has details of the registered keeper (who is not necessarily the legal owner) and the pink section is sent to the DVLA in the UK when the bike is sold. A small section in yellow deals with selling within the motor trade.

In the UK the DVLA will provide details of earlier keepers of the bike upon payment of a small fee, and much can be learned in this way.

If the bike has a foreign registration there may be expensive and time-consuming formalities to complete. Do you really want the hassle? More recently, many of the thousands of Tigers and Daytonas exported to the USA have been re-imported to the UK. Reimporting sounds like a great chance to buy a Triumph that has only been used on dry, West Coast roads, with the added glamour of US heritage. Plus, US prices tend to be lower.

However, if the bike is still in the USA, you'll have to buy it sight unseen, and the paperwork involved in importing and re-registering is a daunting prospect. That means employing a shipping agent; you'll also have to budget in the shipping costs. Then there's (at the time of writing) 6% import duty on the bike and shipping costs, then 20% VAT on the whole lot. Unless you're after a rare US-only spec bike such as a TR5A/R, it's not worth the hassle.

Roadworthiness certificate

Most country/state administrations require that bikes are regularly tested to prove that they are safe to use on the public highway. In the UK that test (the 'MoT') is carried out at approved testing stations, for a fee. In the USA the requirement varies, but most states insist on an emissions test every two years as a minimum, while the police are charged with pulling over unsafe-looking vehicles.

In the UK the test is required on an annual basis for all post-1960 vehicles of more than three years old. Even if it isn't a legal necessity, a conscientious owner can opt to put the bike through the test anyway, as a health check. Of particular relevance for older bikes is that the certificate issued includes the mileage reading recorded at the test date and, therefore, becomes an independent record of that machine's history. Ask the seller if previous certificates are available. Without an MoT the bike should be trailered to its new home, unless you insist that a valid MoT is part of the deal. (Not such a bad idea this, as at least you will know the bike was roadworthy on the day it was tested and you don't need to wait for the old certificate to expire before having the test done.)

Road licence

The administration of every country/state charges some kind of tax for the use of its road system, the actual form of the 'road licence' and, how it is displayed, varying enormously country to country and state to state.

Whatever the form of the road licence, it must relate to the vehicle carrying it and must be present and valid if the bike is to be ridden on the public highway legally. The value of the license will depend on the length of time it will continue to be valid.

In the UK if a bike is untaxed because it has not been used for a period of time, the owner has to inform the licensing authorities, otherwise the vehicle's date-related registration number will be lost and there will be a painful amount of paperwork to get it re-registered. Also in the UK, bikes built before 1st January 1974 (which includes all of the C series Triumphs, even if they weren't first registered until after that date) are road tax exempt. They still had to display a valid paper disc until 1st October 2014, when these were abolished.

Certificates of authenticity

For many makes of classic bike it is possible to get a certificate proving the age and authenticity (eg engine and frame numbers, paint colour and trim) of a particular machine. These are sometimes called 'Heritage Certificates' and if the bike comes with one of these it is a definite bonus. If you want to obtain one, the owners' club is the best starting point.

Valuation certificate

Hopefully, the vendor will have a recent valuation certificate, or letter signed by a recognised expert stating how much he, or she, believes the particular bike to be worth (such documents, together with photos, are usually needed to get 'agreed value' insurance). Generally, such documents should act only as confirmation of your own assessment of the bike rather than a guarantee of value as the expert has probably not seen it in the flesh. The easiest way to find out how to obtain a formal valuation is to contact the owners' club.

Service history

Often these bikes will have been serviced at home by enthusiastic (and hopefully capable) owners for a good number of years. Nevertheless, try to obtain as much service history and other paperwork pertaining to the bike as you can. Naturally specialist garage receipts score most points in the value stakes. However, anything helps in the great authenticity game: items like the original bill of sale, handbook, parts invoices and repair bills add to the story and the character of the machine. Even a brochure correct to the year of the bike's manufacture is a useful document and something that you could well have to search hard to locate in future years. If the seller claims that the bike has been restored, then expect receipts and other evidence from a specialist restorer.

If the seller claims to have carried out regular servicing, ask what work was completed, when, and seek some evidence of it being carried out. Your assessment of the bike's overall condition should tell you whether the seller's claims are genuine.

Restoration photographs

If the seller tells you that the bike has been restored, then expect to be shown a series of photographs taken while the restoration was under way. Pictures taken at various stages, and from various angles, should help you gauge the thoroughness of the work. If you buy the bike, ask if you can have copies of all the photographs as they form an important part of its history.

12 What's it worth?

– let your head rule your heart

Condition

If the bike you've been looking at is really ratty, then you've probably not bothered to use the marking system in chapter 9 – 30 minute evaluation. You may not have even got as far as using that chapter at all!

If you did use the marking system you'll know whether the bike is in excellent (maybe concours), good, average or poor condition or, perhaps, somewhere in between these categories.

To keep up to date with prices, buy the latest editions of the classic bike magazines and check the classified and dealer ads, both in the magazines and online – these are particularly useful as they enable you to compare private and dealer prices. Most of the magazines run auction reports as well, which publish the actual selling prices, as do the auction house websites. Remember that the price listed for online auctions (unless it's a 'Buy it Now' price) is only the highest current bid, not the final selling price.

C series Triumphs are sought after bikes, so bargains are rare, though they are still cheaper than the bigger twins, especially the Bonneville. Late Daytonas and T100Cs tend to fetch the highest prices, as they have all the mechanical/electrical improvements. A 3TA or 5TA with all its original tinwork will also command a decent price.

Bear in mind that a bike that is a recent show winner could be worth more than the highest price usually seen. Assuming that the bike you have in mind is not in show/concours condition, then relate the level of condition that you judge it to be in with the appropriate price in the adverts. How does the figure compare with the asking price?

Before you start haggling with the seller, consider what effect any variation from standard specification might have on the bike's value. This is a personal thing: for some, absolute originality is non-negotiable, while others see non-standard parts as an opportunity to pick up a bargain. Do your research in the reference books, so that you know the bike's spec when it left the factory. That way, you shouldn't end up paying a top-dollar price for a non-original bike. If you are buying from a dealer, remember prices are generally higher than in private sales.

Striking a deal

Negotiate on the basis of your condition assessment, mileage, and fault rectification cost. Also take into account the bike's specification. Be realistic about the value, but don't be completely intractable: a small compromise on the part of the vendor or buyer will often facilitate a deal at little real cost.

13 Do you really want to restore?
– it'll take longer and cost more than you think

With some restoration projects, things can only get better ...

There's a romance about restoration projects, about bringing a sick bike back to blooming health, and it's tempting to buy something that 'just needs a few small jobs' to bring it up to scratch. But there are two things to think about: one, once you've got the bike home and start taking it apart, those few small jobs could turn into big ones. And, two, restoration takes time, which is a precious thing in itself. Be honest with yourself – will you get as much pleasure from working on the bike as you will from riding it?

Achieving this sort of finish can take a long time.

This side panel looks a bit untidy, and it's non-standard – but perfectly usable.

Of course, you could hand over the whole lot to a professional, where the biggest cost involved is not the new parts, but the labour involved. Such restorations don't come cheap, and if taking this route, there are four other issues to bear in mind.

First, make it absolutely clear what you want doing. Do you want the bike to be 100% original at the end of the process, or simply usable? Do you want a concours finish, or are you prepared to put up with a few blemishes on the original parts?

Second, make sure that not only is a detailed estimate involved, but that it is more or less binding. There are too many stories

Minor oil leaks like this are unsightly, but won't stop you using the bike.

of a person quoted one figure only to be presented with an invoice for a far larger one!

Third, check that the company you're dealing with has a good reputation – the owners' club, or one of the reputable parts suppliers, should be able to make a few recommendations.

Finally, having a Triumph 350/500 professionally restored is unlikely to make financial sense as it's likely to cost more than the finished bike will be worth. Not that this should put you off, if you have the budget, and really want to do it this way.

Restoring the bike yourself requires a number of skills, which is fine if you already have them, but if you haven't it's good not to make your newly acquired bike part of the learning curve! Can you weld? Are you confident about building up an engine? Do you have a warm, well-lit garage with a solid workbench and good selection of tools?

Be prepared for a top-notch professional to put you on a lengthy waiting list or, if tackling a restoration yourself, expect things to go wrong and set aside extra time to complete the task. Restorations can stretch into years when things like life intrude, so it's good to have some sort of target date.

There's a lot to be said for a rolling restoration, especially as the summers start to pass with your bike still off the road. This is not the way to achieve a concours finish, which can only really be achieved via a thorough nut-and-bolt rebuild, without the bike getting wet, gritty and salty in the meantime, but an 'on-the-go' restoration does have its plus points. Riding helps keep your interest up as the bike's condition improves, and it's also more affordable than trying to do everything in one go. In the long run, it will take longer, but you'll get some on-road fun out of the bike in the meantime.

14 Paint problems
– bad complexion, including dimples, pimples and bubbles

Paint faults generally occur due to lack of protection/maintenance, or to poor preparation prior to a respray or touch-up. Some of the following conditions may be present in the bike you're looking at:

Orange peel
This appears as an uneven paint surface, similar to the appearance of the skin of an orange. The fault is caused by the failure of atomised paint droplets to flow into each other when they hit the surface. It's sometimes possible to rub out the effect with proprietary paint cutting/rubbing compound or very fine grades of abrasive paper. A respray may be necessary in severe cases. Consult a paint shop for advice.

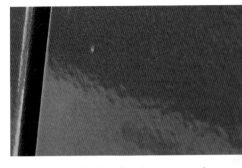

You may be able to rub out orange peel, but in severe cases a respray could be required.

Cracking
Severe cases are likely to have been caused by too heavy an application of paint (or filler beneath the paint). Also, insufficient stirring of the paint before application can lead to the components being improperly mixed, and cracking can result. Incompatibility with the paint already on the panel can have a similar effect. To rectify it is necessary to rub down to a smooth, sound finish before respraying the problem area.

Crazing
Sometimes the paint takes on a crazed rather than a cracked appearance when the problems mentioned under 'cracking' are present. This problem can also be caused by a reaction between the underlying surface and the paint.

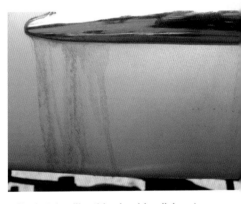

Fuel stains like this should polish out.

Paint removal and respraying the problem area is usually the only solution.

Blistering
Almost always caused by corrosion of the metal beneath the paint. Usually perforation will be found in the metal and the damage will often be worse than that suggested by the area of blistering. The metal will have to be repaired before repainting.

Touching-in the tank badges isn't a big job, but it makes a big difference.

Micro blistering

Usually the result of an economy respray where inadequate heating has allowed moisture to settle on the vehicle before spraying. Consult a paint specialist, but damaged paint will have to be removed before partial or full respraying. Can also be caused by bike covers that don't 'breathe.'

Fading

Some colours, especially reds, are prone to fading if subject to strong sunlight for long periods without the benefit of polish protection. Sometimes proprietary paint restorers and/or paint cutting/rubbing compounds will retrieve the situation. Often a respray is the only real solution.

Peeling

Often a problem with metallic paintwork when the sealing lacquer becomes damaged and begins to peel off. Poorly applied paint may also peel. The remedy is to strip and start again.

Dimples

Dimples in the paintwork are caused by the residue of polish (particularly silicone types) not being removed properly before respraying. Paint removal and repainting is the only solution.

There's a tiny blemish below the badge on this Tiger 90, but it's been there a long time ...

15 Problems due to lack of use
– just like their owners, Triumph twins need exercise!

Like any piece of engineering, and indeed like human beings, Triumph twins deteriorate if they sit doing nothing for long periods. This is especially relevant if the bike is laid up for six months of the year, as some are.

Rust
If the bike is put away wet, and/or stored a cold, damp garage, the paint, metal and brightwork will suffer. Ensure the machine is completely dry and clean before going into storage, and if you can afford it, invest in a dehumidifier to keep the garage atmosphere dry.

Cables
Cables are vulnerable to seizure – the answer is to thoroughly lube them beforehand, and come into the garage to give them a couple of pulls once a week or so.

Tyres
If the bike's been left on its sidestand, most of its weight is on the tyres, which will develop flat spots

A dry, well ventilated workshop is better than a damp shed for long-term storage.

and cracks over time. Always leave the bike on its centre stand, if there is one, which takes weight off the tyres.

Rubber, whether tyres or tank mountings, deteriorates over time.

Engine

Old, acidic oil can corrode bearings. Many riders change the oil in the spring, when they're putting the bike back on the road, but really it should be changed just before the bike is laid up, so that the bearings are sitting in fresh oil. The same goes for the gearbox. While you're giving the cables their weekly exercise, turn the engine over slowly on the kickstart, ignition off. Don't start it though – running the engine for a short time does more harm than good, as it produces a lot of moisture internally, which the engine doesn't get hot enough to burn off. That will attack the engine internals and the silencers.

Battery/electrics

Either remove the battery and give it a top-up charge every couple of weeks, or connect it up to a battery top-up device such as the Optimate, which will keep it permanently fully charged. Damp conditions will allow fuses and earth connections to corrode, storing up electrical troubles for the spring. Eventually, wiring insulation will harden and fail.

Give the levers a pull once a week – this is a Bonneville, but the same principle applies.

VISIT VELOCE ON THE WEB – WWW.VELOCE.CO.UK
All current books • New book news • Special offers • Gift vouchers • Forum

Auctioneers

Bonhams www.bonhams.com
Cheffins www.cheffins.co.uk
eBay www.eBay.com
H&H www.classic-auctions.co.uk
Silver www.silverauctions.

Clubs across the world

Triumph Owners Motorcycle Club
The original and longest-lived Triumph
club. Offers a bike dating service.
www.tomcc.org

Triumph Owners Motorcycle Club –
Germany
www.tmoc.de

Triumph Owners Motorcycle Club –
New Zealand
www.tomcc.co.nz

Triumph International Owners Club –
USA
www.tioc.org

Triumph Owners Motorcycle Club –
Denmark
www.triumphmc.dk

Triumph Owners Motorcycle Club –
Netherlands
www.triumphownersclub.nl

Triumph Owners Motorcycle Club –
Norway
www.tomcc-n.com

Triumph Owners Motorcycle Club –
Australia
PO Box 257, Belgrave, 3160
www.tomcc.com.au

Triumph Owners Motorcycle Club –
Sweden
www.tomccsweden.se

Club Triton – France
www.triton-france.com

Specialists

There are so many Triumph twin
specialists out there that it would
be impossible to list them all, so
we have restricted our listing to UK
companies. This list does not imply
recommendation, and is not deemed to
be comprehensive.

Britbits
Spares – Bournemouth
www.britbits.co.uk
01202 483675

Camelford Bike Bits
Spares – Cornwall
01840 213483

Cheney Racing
Spares (for Cheney frames)
www.cheneyracing.co.uk
07789 170587

Electrex World
Ignition/electrical parts
www.electrexworld.co.uk
01491 682369

MS Motorcycles
Paint and dating service
www.msmotorcyclesuk.com
07773 296826

Kidderminster Motorcycles
Spares – Herefordshire
01562 66679

Kirby Rowbotham
Electronic ignition/oil filters – Staffordshire
www.kirbyrowbotham.com
01889 584758

Morgo
Uprated oil pumps
www.morgo.co.uk

Reg Allen
Spares – London
www.reg-allen-london.co.uk
020 8579 1248

Robin James Engineering
Restorations – Herefordshire
www.robinjamesengineering.com
01568 612800

Rockerbox
Spares – Surrey
www.rockerbox.co.uk
01252 722973

SRM Engineering
Spares/engineering – Aberystwyth
www.srm-engineering.com
01970 627771

The Bike Shed
Restorations/servicing – Hertfordshire
www.inventivestudios.co.uk/thebikeshed
07807 828917

Tri-Cor England
Spares – Herefordshire
www.tri-corengland.com
 01432 820752

Tri-Supply
Spares – Devon
www.trisupply.co.uk
01395 444099

Unity Equipe
Spares – Lancashire
www.unityequipe.com
01706 839059

History/general
www.triumph-tiger-90.com &
www.triumph-tiger-100.com
Lots of useful information on up-to-1968
models.

Books
These books are currently out of print,
but secondhand copies are available to
buy online.

British Motorcycles Since 1950
Vols 5 & 6
Steve Wilson, PSL 1992

Triumph Twenty-one to Daytona
Matthew Vale, Crowood Press, 2008

Triumph Twin Restoration
Roy Bacon, Osprey, 1985

Triumph Twins & Triples
Roy Bacon, Osprey, 1981

17 Vital statistics

– essential data at your fingertips

Listing the vital statistics of every C series variant would take far more room than we have here, so we've picked three representative models: 1958 Twenty-one, 1966 T100SS and 1968 Daytona T100R.

Max speed

1958 Twenty-one – 82mph
1966 T100SS – 98mph
1968 Daytona – 105mph

Engine

1958 Twenty-one – Air-cooled vertical twin – 349cc. Bore and stroke 58.25 x 65.5mm. Compression ratio 7.5:1. 18.5bhp @ 6,500rpm
1966 T100SS – Air-cooled vertical twin – 490cc. Bore and stroke 69 x 65.5mm. Compression ratio 9.0:1. 34bhp @ 7000rpm
1968 Daytona – Air-cooled vertical twin – 490cc. Bore and stroke 69 x 65.5mm. Compression ratio 9.0:1. 41bhp @ 7400rpm

Gearbox

1958 Twenty-one – Four-speed. Ratios: 1st 13.0:1, 2nd 9.32:1, 3rd 6.30:1, 4th 5.31:1.
1966 T100SS – Four-speed. Ratios: 1st 14.09:1, 2nd 9.18:1, 3rd 6.95:1, 4th 5.70:1
1968 Daytona – Four-speed. Ratios 1st 14.39:1, 2nd 9.38:1, 3rd 7.11:1, 4th 5.82:1

Brakes

1958 Twenty-one – Cable, 7in front drum, 7in rear drum
1966 T100SS – Cable, 7in front drum, 7in rear drum
1968 Daytona – Cable, 7in twin-leading shoe front drum, 7in rear drum

Electrics

1958 Twenty-one – 6-volt, alternator
1966 T100SS – 12-volt, alternator
1968 Daytona – 12-volt, alternator

Weight

1958 Twenty-one – 340lb
1966 T100SS – 337lb
1968 Daytona – 340lb

Major change points by model year

1957 Twenty-one launched
1959 5TA launched, Twenty-one renamed 3TA
1960 T100A launched
1961 TR5AR and TR5AC launched, steering head angle changed
1962 T100SS replaces T100A with bikini side panels
1963 T90 launched, twin cb points ignition

1964 External-spring forks, Tigers drop all panelling, 3TA/5TA have bikini

1965 Stiffening top tube on frame, longer-travel forks

1966 12-volt electrics, 'eyebrow' tank badges, stiffer frame

1967 Daytona launched with stronger, lighter frame

1968 Forks with shuttle-valve damping, Lucas 6CA cb points, Amal Concentric carbs

1969 Stronger bottom end with ball-race timing side main bearing, 'Triumph' logo stamped on engine number, oil pressure warning light, Lucas RM21 alternator, 8in TLS front brake for Daytona, 7in TLS for the others

1970 New crankcase breathing to reduce oil leaks

1971 New switchgear and indicators, black-faced instruments

1972 Push-in exhaust downpipes

1973 TR5T launched to replace T100C

1974/75 Final Daytonas and TR5Ts sold off

Engine/frame numbers

Production for each model year began in August. That is, 1969 model bikes began rolling off the lines in August 1968, after the summer holidays:

1957 H1 to H760

1958 H761 to H5480

1959 H5481 to H11511

1960 H11512 to H18611

1961 H18612 to H25251

1962 H25252 to H29732

1963 H29733 to H32464

1964 H32465 to H35986

1965 H35987 to H40527

1966 H40528 to H48728

1967 H48729 to H57082

1968 H57083 to H65572

1969 H65573 to H67331 (now stamped over a background of Triumph logos)

After 1969 the engine numbering system changes to a mixture of letters and numbers indicating month and year of manufacture:

C	1969	**A**	January
D	1970	**B**	February
E	1971	**C**	March
G	1972	**D**	April
H	1973	**E**	May
J	1974	**F**	June
K	1975	**G**	July
N	1976	**J**	August
		K	September
		N	October
		P	November
		X	December

Model codes

Stamped to the left of the engine/frame numbers. WD = Army, P = Police, W= Radio-equipped.

T21	1957-58	**T100SC**	1963-68
3TA	1959-66	**T100SR**	1963-66
5TA	1959-66	**T100**	1965
T100A	1959-62	**T100C**	1966-72
TR5AR	1961-62	**T100R**	1967-74
TR5AC	1961-62	**T100S**	1968
T90	1962-68	**T100T**	1967-74
T100SS	1962-70	**TR5T**	1973-74

The Essential Buyer's Guide™ series ...

The Essential Buyer's Guide
BUS

978-1-
845840-22-8

The Essential Buyer's Guide
TR6

978-1-
845840-26-6

The Essential Buyer's Guide
MGB
MGB GT

978-1-
845840-29-7

The Essential Buyer's Guide
E-type

978-1-
845840-77-8

The Essential Buyer's Guide
2CV

978-1-
845840-99-0

The Essential Buyer's Guide
PORSCHE
928

978-1-
904788-70-6

The Essential Buyer's Guide
MINOR & 1000

978-1-
845841-01-0

The Essential Buyer's Guide
XJ6, XJ12
& Sovereign

978-1-
845841-19-5

The Essential Buyer's Guide
230, 250 & 280SL

978-1-
845841-13-3

The Essential Buyer's Guide
GS

978-1-
845841-35-5

The Essential Buyer's Guide
500 & 650 Twins

978-1-
845841-36-2

The Essential Buyer's Guide
DS & ID

978-1-
845841-38-6

The Essential Buyer's Guide
SILVER SHADOW
& T-SERIES

978-1-
845841-46-1

The Essential Buyer's Guide
500 & 600

978-1-
845841-47-8

The Essential Buyer's Guide
IMPREZA

978-1-
845841-63-8

The Essential Buyer's Guide
Bantam

978-1-
845841-65-2

The Essential Buyer's Guide
GOLF GTI

978-1-
845841-88-1

The Essential Buyer's Guide
XJ40

978-1-
845841-92-8

The Essential Buyer's Guide
XJ

978-1-
845842-00-0

The Essential Buyer's Guide
MINI

978-1-
845842-04-8

The Essential Buyer's Guide
CAPRI

978-1-
845842-05-5

The Essential Buyer's Guide
STAG

978-1-
845842-70-3

The Essential Buyer's Guide
Commando

978-1-
845842-81-9

The Essential Buyer's Guide
205 GTI

978-1-
845842-83-3

The Essential Buyer's Guide
SOHC FOURS

978-1-
845842-84-0

The Essential Buyer's Guide
TRIPLES & FOURS

978-1-
845842-87-1

The Essential Buyer's Guide
BONNEVILLE

978-1-84584-
134-8

The Essential Buyer's Guide
Big Twins

978-1-
845843-03-8

The Essential Buyer's Guide
CBR600
HURRICANE

978-1-
845843-09-0

The Essential Buyer's Guide
TR7 & TR8

978-1-
845843-16-8

The Essential Buyer's Guide
CORVETTE

978-1-
845843-29-8

The Essential Buyer's Guide
911SC

978-1-
845843-30-4

The Essential Buyer's Guide
SCOOTERS

978-1-
845843-34-2

The Essential Buyer's Guide
911 (964)

978-1-
845843-38-0

The Essential Buyer's Guide
911 (996)

978-1-
845843-39-7

The Essential Buyer's Guide
XJ-S

978-1-
845841-61-4

The Essential Buyer's Guide
MX-5 MIATA

978-1-
845842-31-4

The Essential Buyer's Guide
CBR FireBlade

978-1-
845843-07-6

The Essential Buyer's Guide
911 (993)

978-1-
845843-40-3

The Essential Buyer's Guide
SERIES I, II & IIA

978-1-
845843-48-9

The Essential Buyer's Guide
Bevel Twins

978-1-
845843-63-2

The Essential Buyer's Guide
924

978-1-
845844-09-7

... don't buy a vehicle until you've read one of these!

978-1-845843-52-6   978-1-845846-55-8   978-1-845847-55-5   978-1-845843-54-0   978-1-845843-92-2   978-1-845843-59-5   978-1-845843-60-1

978-1-845847-56-2   978-1-845843-77-9   978-1-845843-91-5   978-1-845844-42-4   978-1-845845-23-0   978-1-845843-95-3   978-1-845844-08-0

978-1-845844-21-9   978-1-845844-22-6   978-1-845844-23-3   978-1-845844-24-0   978-1-845844-30-1   978-1-845844-34-9   978-1-845845-25-4

978-1-845844-43-1   978-1-845844-45-5   978-1-845844-47-9   978-1-845844-56-1   978-1-845844-62-2   978-1-845844-86-8   978-1-845844-87-5

978-1-845845-26-1   978-1-904788-69-0   978-1-845845-33-9   978-1-904788-72-0   978-1-904788-85-0   978-1-845846-09-1   978-1-845844-86-8

978-1-904788-98-0   978-1-845845-71-1   978-1-845846-14-5   978-1-845841-07-2

£9.99 – £12.99 / $19.95
(prices subject to change, p&p extra).

For more details visit
www.veloce.co.uk
or email info@veloce.co.uk

Also from Veloce Publishing ...

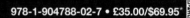

– Harry Woolridge –

THE TRIUMPH TROPHY BIBLE

Including unit-construction Trophy-based TIGER models

– Harry Woolridge –

THE TRIUMPH SPEED TWIN & THUNDERBIRD BIBLE

All 5T 498cc & 6T 649cc models 1938 to 1966

978-1-904788-02-7 • £35.00/$69.95*

978-1-904788-26-3 • £30.00/$59.95*

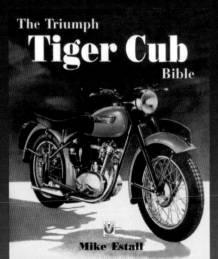

The Triumph **Tiger Cub** Bible

Mike Estall

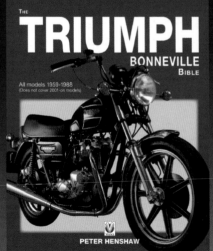

THE **TRIUMPH** BONNEVILLE BIBLE

All models 1959-1988
(Does not cover 2001-on models)

PETER HENSHAW

978-1-904788-09-6 • £50.00/$79.95*

978-1-845843-98-4 • £35.00/$54.95*

For more info on Veloce titles, visit our website at www.veloce.co.uk
email: info@veloce.co.uk • Tel: +44(0)1305 260068
*prices subject to change, p&p extra

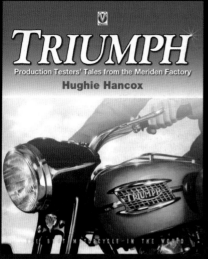

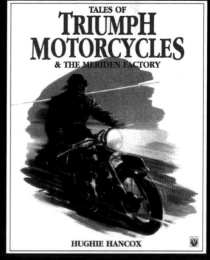

978-1-845844-41-7 • £19.99/$39.95*

978-1-901295-67-2 • £24.99/$39.95*

978-1-845842-65-9 • £12.49/$24.95*

For more info on Veloce titles, visit our website at www.veloce.co.uk
email: info@veloce.co.uk • Tel: +44(0)1305 260068
* prices subject to change, p&p extra

Index